MW00901702

A is for APPLE.
Let's take a bite.

B is for BALL.
They're round and tight.

C is for CARING,
for everything you like.

D is for DOGS
that bark in the night.

E is for EAGLE.
We'll watch them take flight.

F is for FOX
because they can see
at night.

G is for GOATS
who chew with all their might.

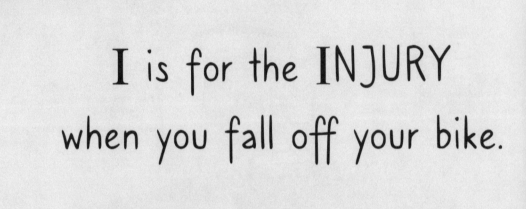

I is for the INJURY
when you fall off your bike.

J is for JUPITER,
the fifth planet with stripe

K is for KANGAROO.
Watch them hop 'til midnight.

L is for LOVE.
We embrace it with might.

M is for MONKEY...
because they're alright.

N is for NO,
meaning all the things we dislike.

O is for OUT,
and you point to the right.

P is for the PIG
who eat with delight.

Q is for QUIET
so you can sleep tonight.

R is for RUN...
when there is danger in sight.

S is for SAFETY
to ensure you're alright.

T is for TWINS
that may look alike.

U is for UNDERSTANDING
because you're a delight.

V is for VICTORY
and being polite.

W is for WOODS,
for those who like to hike.

X is for the XYLOPHONE,
with its sound so light.

Y is for YELLOW,
a color that's so bright.

Z is for the ZOOKEEPERS
who all dress alike!

The End

CPSIA information can be obtained
at www.ICGtesting.com
Printed in the USA
LVHW072115200521
688036LV00004B/18